Buy a Life Insurance Policy to Secure Your Family's Financial Future

Peter K. Black

To my readers and my wonderful wife

Table of Contents

WHY EVEN DISCUS LIFE INSURANCE?

The National Safety Council data in 2008 recorded that a disabling injury occurs every second on and off the job.[1] This has led to the rise in wage and productivity losses due to unintentional injuries to $364 billion in 2013.[2] Every thirty 30 seconds, someone files bankruptcy due to a disabling illness.[3] The Council for Disability Awareness says that over 1 in 4 of today's 20 year olds will become disabled before they retire.[4]

The reasons and causes for the statistics are many – it does not always have to be carelessness. Simple mistakes could result into accidents, and humans are not immune to making mistakes. That is part of being human. Reason why we take pains training people in our companies to do their work properly, and to use machinery and equipment in the right way. Information and training helps us do things instinctively without much though.

We all hope no such accident or critical illness befall any of our family members. Accidents and illnesses can throw surprises and wreak havoc on our finances. The next best thing is to be prepared at all times. So we mention the statistics not to create fear, but to educate people and hopefully see informed choices done.

Information should instead spur people to act and take precautionary measures. If something happens to you, are you prepared financially? Will your family survive without going bankrupt? No one relishes facing these questions, much less answer them. But these are real questions that need to be answered and addressed. Even if the answers are painful.

Financial preparation may seem daunting with the rising cost of daily living and all the risks we face on a daily basis. It becomes all the more scary when we consider how even what was considered an institution in the financial world crumbled in 2008. How can we be sure our investments are safe, sound, and secure for when we really need them? Which financial instrument is safest to invest in right now?

The answer is still basic information. Understanding what financial instrument fits each need, desire, or goal is key to investing. Each investment also come with risks associated with it. Risk is everywhere and they cannot be avoided, but they can be managed properly. After all, the need to save up for emergencies does not go away just because the financial world has a lot of challenges. You are still aging every minute of every day. Soon, you will have to think of your retirement plan, if you haven't started yet. You see, the presence of financial risk to investments does not remove nor override the reasons for our need to secure our future.

WHAT INSURANCE IS

Life insurance is a form of security for your loved ones. This financial instrument entails a person enter a policy contract and pay an agreed-upon premium for life insurance coverage. This coverage is the amount paid to the beneficiaries of the insured upon death of the insured.

What makes this coverage so important? When the insured dies, his income contribution to the family also stops. No one wishes this to happen, and you certainly don't know if it will happen to you, but it does happen to people. The payment that will be provided by a life insurance policy is, in effect, a form of replacement for the lost income contribution of the insured to his family. Having such a benefit ensures that the beneficiaries will be able to continue life without suffering financial hardship or bankruptcy.

Income replacement is the reason why insurance is very popular among those who have minor dependents. Minor children are not able to work for themselves yet; thus, parents find it necessary to have some assurance for their kids' future in case something happens to them before their kids reach the legal working age. Death may not necessarily be the result of an accident, but disability and dismemberment are distinct probabilities. Death, disability, or dismemberment – it all boils down to loss of income.

But income replacement is not the only raison d'etre of insurance for those savvy in financial instruments. The rich and affluent also make use of insurance as part of estate planning, which is simply put, wise management of resources. It is high time we learn from the rich and benefit from prudent practices with our finances.

DIFFERENT KINDS OF LIFE INSURANCE

There are different types of life insurance products available in the market today. While the basic purpose of a life insurance as an instrument for financial security remains the same, life insurance offerings have evolved to meet the changing needs of people.

It is simply like the question working women face every day when choosing what to wear – is it skirt or pants today? Rugged, corporate, or smart casual? Conservative, faddish, or classic? In the end, the answers to the choices will boil down to function – will the work entail running out on field for meetings? Whom will I be meeting with today, junior officers or top executives?

To some people, the variety of insurance product available in the market has made things confusing. The good thing is that insurance may be given different labels according to their product type, but there are only a few generic types you should remember, and each fills a specific need.

Term Life Insurance

Term life insurance is perhaps most commonly encountered type of life insurance by working people, especially back in the years when life insurance was always among the benefits provided by companies. Companies in the manufacturing sector commonly provide this kind of insurance as an added benefit to their employees because the existence of heavy machinery in the workplace doubles the risk exposure of humans. By providing a term life insurance benefit, companies actually avoid having to spend more in cases of accidents.

This kind of insurance generally comes with a fixed rate of premium, for a specific amount of life coverage, within a specified time frame. The time frame may be anywhere from five to 20 years. Yearly renewable group term life insurance is likewise common. It is this annual renewal feature that makes this the most sensible and cost-effective for companies to provide their employees.

The annual premium must be paid in order to keep the term life insurance in force. If the insured misses the payment, the insurance automatically lapses. This kind of insurance has no cash value whatsoever. It only offers a lump-sum benefit to the insured's beneficiary.

What makes term life insurance attractive for groups of people such as company employees is the low rates for the annual premium. Generally, the amount of premium goes down as the number of group members increase. By getting term life insurance for their employees, companies are effectively shielding them from the high cost of accidents at work. In addition, giving term life insurance as a benefit gives a company a positive image with its workers.

What's the lowdown? This insurance may only be enjoyed by the employees while they are still with the company. Remember, the pricing given by the insurance company was packaged for the specific number of employees and benefits incorporated in the group insurance they got. Insurance providers make their corporate clients accountable on a yearly basis, and accept employees only as members of the group for the group rate. Some insurance providers, however, have added the feature of including dependents of corporate clients' employees for the group rate, subject to certain requirements.

So when an employee leaves the company, they can no longer subscribe to the same term life insurance policy even if they wanted to pay it on their own. The only way to enjoy the protection afforded by insurance after one has left the company is to get an individual policy.

In some cases, depending on the product and the insurance provider, the term life insurance taken while in a company may be converted into a permanent life insurance policy. This will, however, have different benefits and premium amount from the group term life you previously got.

The details starting to make you sleepy? Fortunately, you don't have to worry about term life insurance for your company. These things are decided on by the human resources department of companies, and the employees themselves are spared from all the hassle of negotiating for the benefits they will get. If you are an employee with a term life insurance as benefit from your company, all you have to do is let your personnel department process any claim in your behalf. No sweat!

Whole Life Insurance

A permanent life insurance policy is called a **whole life insurance.** This kind of insurance provides lifetime coverage, and is normally more expensive than term life insurance. The higher premium of this kind of insurance is due to the higher protection coverage it gives to the insured, and *lifetime coverage* is defined as *being insured up to 99 years of age.*

There is nothing to worry about paying exorbitant fees though. The amount of insurance coverage will be computed by your financial advisor, and is dependent on your financial resources and needs. There is no fixed price, the products are flexible, and designed to enable adjustments according to client's specifications. Life insurance is a medium- to long-term investment. Your financial advisor will help you map out a financial plan for you that will not jeopardize your budget to meet your present needs and have an emergency fund as well.

You even get to decide what *riders* to get along with the main life insurance. Riders are like side dishes to your main viand. In this case, the main viand is the life insurance coverage. There are many choices provided for your rider, and some will also be discussed in a later section.

Aside from the higher premiums, whole life insurance may also come with cash value. This cash value may be a savings component, or an amount from which one may take a loan. As a cash component, it becomes akin to your savings account in the bank with some differences. Savings incorporated in an insurance product is meant for your medium- to long-term goals, while your bank deposits are for meant to meet your short-term needs.

At other times, the value placed on your life insurance policy is called *account value*, and is not like the cash value at all. It merely is the value given for any loan that you may take from your insurance policy. It is considered a loan because your policy contract indicates a benefit to your beneficiaries only upon death of insured. So any cash taken from the policy while the insured is still alive is actually a borrowed amount from what should be received by your beneficiaries at a later date.

Whatever loan you take from your whole life insurance policy is just like any loan that has an interest, and has to be paid. In case the loan is not paid and the insured dies, the loan will simply be deducted from the proceeds that will be given to your beneficiary.

The features of a *whole life insurance* product may vary from one product to another, or from one service to another. The most important thing to remember is that it provides a lifetime coverage for the insured.

People who have term life insurance provided by their employers are often lulled into a deceiving contentment with having just their term life insurance. This should not be so. If you can afford to get your own life insurance policy, I strongly encourage you to do so.

Companies normally get the barest minimum of benefit to cover accident expenses and to help a little with burial expenses in case of death. But a term life insurance that comes as a benefit from your company is seldom sufficient to replace your income should anything happen to you. Company-provided term life insurance is often offered with standard benefits for employees in the same category level. But your needs may be different from those of your co-workers, even if they are on the same category as you are. Definitely your dreams and goals for your family are distinct to you. That's why you need a life insurance policy tailor-fit for your needs, resources, and goals for yourself and your family.

Universal Variable Life Insurance

In recent years, a new variation of insurance has been brought to the market. The **universal variable life insurance** incorporates an investment component along with the insurance protection coverage.

These products generally have a lower insurance component than *whole life insurance*. Premium payments are automatically divided according to the investment options taken by the client when the policy is started.

Insurance providers normally present an array of investment fund options for the client. The choices may include investment in bonds, fixed income securities, stocks, or a balanced fund. The array of investments ensures that the needs of people will be served regardless of their risk appetite.

For those who want to simply have a stable income from their universal life insurance, bonds or fixed income securities will be the best. But for the bold and daring, stock funds hold the allure because it offers the highest potential income. Higher interest income means higher risks.

Insurance products that are invested in mutual funds offer a distinct advantage over investing in stocks and bonds on your own. Imagine thousands of people investing different amounts in a mutual fund. This fund is managed by a professional management team, and has its own team doing research to aid the fund manager who actually takes care of investing the people's money. It takes out the hassle of monitoring and studying trends in the stock exchange. Its just like living the life of a billionaires who have staff who ensures the money of the *Don* earns.

Moreover, if you are a small investor, you get to ride on the growth of the pooled money of investors, enabling you to earn even from blue chip stocks which you may not necessarily afford on your own. On top of that, a mutual fund is fully diversified, with most funds holding stocks of up to 30 different listed companies. That means whatever downturn in some stocks may occur, there will be other stocks in the basket that will keep steady, and even increase, the value of your investment.

Insurance is far from boring. This kind of insurance is commonly used to fill medium- to long-term goals of people, whatever their goal may be. Financial planning today is a step to financial freedom tomorrow.

Riders

So what are the riders thrown into the basic life insurance coverage by your Financial Advisor? Simply to add more commission to their sale? True protection benefits? Are they necessary? These questions are natural, so no need to be ashamed about them. It is good to ask questions and understand every nook and cranny of your investment.

Riders are optional benefits which may be included in the basic life protection benefit of your policy. As mentioned earlier, accidents may not necessarily cause death. Some people survive accidents but are left with some impairment or disability. In other cases, disability or impairment may be caused by sickness or disease. Are all these covered by riders?

Since riders are optional, the choice of which rider to include in your basic plan is left up to you. Financial advisors are there to explain which riders may be suited to you and your life situation, but the final say will still be yours. While the riders normally cost lower than the basic life plan, they may still add up to a substantial amount if you pile it all up on your basic life plan. The key is to know the benefits of riders available, and choose what is essential to your specific life case.

The most basic, and often included, rider is the *Accident and Health rider*. This rider gives benefit to disability, or in some products dismemberment, caused by an accident. This is a crucial benefit because not all accidents cause death. Sometimes it just leaves one impaired. If you have this rider and death is caused by an accident, the death benefit could even be double your basic life coverage.

Another important rider is the *waiver of premium.* in case the insured becomes disabled or dismembered in such a way that he is not able to perform his normal work, and he is not yet done with the premium payments, then the insurance provider pays for the remaining premium left unpaid for the insurance policy of the insured.

Some life insurance products have the option to include a rider that gives a benefit for cases of hospitalization due to sickness or disease. The added benefit could come in the form of a daily income for every day spent in the hospital. In most cases, this is paid after filing of proof that the insured has been hospitalized. this is also a good way of defraying any cost that may be incurred in case of hospitalization. However, the rider must be included in your policy before you even get hospitalized. It must all be planned, leaving nothing to chance.

Lately, however, rising cases of terminal or serious illnesses have spawned another innovation to insurance products. HMO cards that are paid on a yearly basis, and with rising cost as you get older, are throw away investments. HMOs are renewed on a yearly basis and offer coverage for as long as you have paid the dues. But they serve a purpose that your life insurance rider may not be able to meet. Working with your financial planner will help you see the best combination to make the most of what you have.

Life insurers nevertheless offer you a benefit for critical illness which an HMO may not provide. A *critical illness rider* gives a predetermined lump sum benefit payment, released upon diagnosis of a critical illness of the insured. The cash benefit is released directly to the insured, making it available for use even for home care and outpatient expenses which are not covered by HMOs.

When taken as a rider benefit, the critical illness rider is cut above HMO benefits. An added benefit is that the rate that you pay for the critical illness rider is locked in at the rate given to you when you got your policy, and it stays the same until the end of your premium payments. So if you get your rider at a young age, chances are the price of your life insurance policy and rider will still be very low.

SO WHO NEEDS LIFE INSURANCE?

Protection for Loved Ones

People normally look for insurance agents when they mark special life events. Marriage, new baby, sickness in someone close to them – there is always an event that triggers *what ifs* in the mind of people for them to go looking for financial advisors, or even to listen to sound financial planning advise. The truth is, no one should wait for life events to start preparing.

The trigger point for those getting married is the thought of financial security for the life they are responsible for. Having a spouse and kids put tremendous pressure on breadwinners. This is heaviest when kids are still infants, and thoughts of how to raise the kid well swarm the mind of the parents. The natural tendency is to look for some form of security as a blanket to cushion any sudden event in life.

Income Replacement

Perhaps the most important question to answer when considering buying a life insurance is your readiness in case of an emergency. Will your family be able to meet immediate expenses to continue their life with a change in income flow brought about by death or disability? If your children are still studying, will they be able to continue their studies? If disability happens to you, do you have a fund set aside for treatment and a back-up plan to go with it?

Although the SSS gives benefit for disability, there is normally a waiting period of six months before any such benefit is released. A back-up plan is necessary in order for you to go through treatment and recover. A life insurance policy with the proper riders could be part of your contingency plan.

High-risk Jobs

Most jobs expose people to a certain risk. The risk may just vary depending on profession. Even the ordinary employees of real estate developers who often go out on field will necessitate an insurance because constant travel increases the risk exposure. People with jobs that expose them to risks should have life insurance. In a number of cases, private companies require contractors to have life or accident insurance for their employees prior to qualifying for any project bid. This is often seen in the construction industry.

The manufacturing sector is filled with high-tech equipments and machineries that may pose risks to labourers. The more industrialized a country gets, the more machineries will be brought in to make production faster and more efficient.

Keyman Insurance

Companies, aside from thinking of term life insurance for employees, also have the option to get a *keyman insurance* for key people in the company. This gives protection benefit to people highly valued by the company for their contribution to the organization.

Estate Planning

Want to be wise like the wealthy? Then consult your financial advisor on how to properly do estate planning. For tax mitigation measures, a life insurance policy may come in handy. Proceeds from life insurance are generally tax free. By investing in life insurance, a person effectively transfer wealth to his heirs with no tax, or lower taxes. There are certain procedures to follow in this, and it will be good to have a trustworthy financial advisor.

PREPARING YOUR FINANCIAL PLAN

The security of our family is foremost on each person's list of priorities. We work hard not just to meet our needs on a daily basis, but even to store up for our future. Nobody wants to work forever, that's why most save up for the time when they could comfortably retire. Ideally, you should also have a fund for emergencies. This is set aside from your everyday expenses.

They say the main problems of a person are: dying too soon, or living too long. What a pathetic way of summing up one's life, right? But it is the reality of living on planet earth. If a person dies too soon, his family members can get caught unprepared with the sudden loss of an income generating unit in the family. Living too long, on the other hand, looms with pictures of huge expenses on homes and medicines. So what do we do?

Where do I Start?

Start with a simple accounting of your monthly household expenses. List down everything you spend on and start being accountable for every penny you have. Normally, you will have to spend one whole month of listing down everything you spend on, so you can see the actual expenses. Transportation, food, groceries, clothes, toiletries, electric bill, phone bill – list down everything.

Don't forget to include every incidental expense such as meals in restaurants and the little shopping trips that you take. The unaccounted for coffee with your hubby, friends, or officemates may be little, but may be eating up a substantial portion of your income.

At the end of the month, do your account balance and see what is left of your income. Did you leave enough money for savings? Health? Emergencies? Recreation? Future tuition of your baby? Travel, perhaps? What, you didn't plan on having fun?

Let's be real for one moment. Perhaps the reason why a lot of people do not invest in insurance is the seriousness of preparing for death. Maybe. Then there is the oft-repeated statement that the benefit of insurance is not on the investor, not on the insured, but on his beneficiaries. Well, back in the days when there was just term life insurance and whole life, that may have been true. But it stopped being true when universal variable insurance came into existence.

The next step will be to set your goals. Draw up your short-term, medium-term, and long-term goals. So start writing down goals now. If you have not started dreaming of what you want to have in life, then start dreaming now! Its never too late to have dreams to work on. Once your goals are written down, then we will match your goals with the right financial vehicles.

First, do you have an emergency fund that you can easily withdraw if ever it is needed? In case you get hospitalized this year, is there a provision for it? Do you have a hospitalization benefit you can count on? If not, then you need to set aside some amount for this.

How about a sudden car breakdown that will not be covered by your car insurance? Or what if your Labrador puppy rips off your cushion in the living room, can you replace it immediately without using a credit card? These are immediate needs that may spring up within the year, and are included in your short-term emergencies.

Your short-term needs must be stored up in an appropriate vehicle. Although it is for your short-term needs, it can still earn a little interest while waiting for you to spend. Bank savings accounts or time deposits will be sufficient for this purpose. This fund is to be set aside, and not touched for everyday expenses.

Next, what would you be needing money for in three to five years time? Will you be in need of a new car to replace your antiquated Beetle? Perhaps you want to travel to another country for a vacation with your family? How much would your vacation cost?

Lastly, will your children be in college in seven years' or ten years' time? it is not part of the culture of America, but wouldn't it be nice to know that you can spend for your kid's college education if you want to? Would you want to live simply, but in style in your sunset years?

Remember, your goals must be measureable and realistic. Your life insurance coverage may need to be bigger while your kids are still very young, and your available money for long-term savings is quite limited. if you are just starting a family, your biggest priority will be to secure the future of your wife and kids, thus, the bigger life insurance coverage. The right product will be a *whole life insurance* as it offers the bigger amount of life protection benefit.

But if your company provides you with a term life insurance benefit, maybe, you can jump to universal variable life insurance and start saving up for your goals. This option is a good choice to take in this case only because you are just adding to the life protection benefit that is already being provided through your term life insurance.

As you progress to a different life stage in a few years time, you may already have added disposable income that may be set aside for medium- to long-term savings. This is when it gets exciting! So what do you want to do in three to five years' time? if its vacation, how much is comfortable for you to save on an annual basis?

Even when you are looking at your future goals, you don't ever neglect your emergency fund. It must be intact, or even increasing and continually earning interest. You can save up for a variety of goals, the choices are limitless. Nothing to worry about! You may have multiple life insurance policies!

You may even set up one universal variable life insurance policy for each life stage you will go through. Yes, its allowed, but you wonder if it is beneficial to do so. The truth is, it is part of estate planning. The money you will leave or give to your kids as inheritance may be passed on through universal life insurance policies. The advantage of doing this is the distinct probability that you bequeath a heritage that may ultimately be tax free. There are intricate legal details to take note of, so get a prudent financial advisor, listen, and act on the advice of your advisor.

Which life insurance provider do I choose?

No one wants to lose their hard-earned money just because a company did not take good care of it. So there are a few practical steps we need to do. It will take you getting involved not just in having a financial plan tailor made for yourself, but in making the company you invest in accountable to its investors as well.

The key is to be informed and stay updated. After all, the presence of financial risk to investments does not remove nor override the reasons for our need to secure our future. So you want your financial security but do not know if any company is safe to invest in after the 2008 financial meltdown? Choose the best companies, known in their field, and transparent to their investors. You also have to make them accountable by giving them feedback.

Contrary to the popular notion, feedback does not have to be in the form of criticism or negativity. The world already has a lot of it now, and does not need any more added. Why not try a positive reinforcement in dealing expressing your evaluation of the pastries at Starbucks the next time you visit?

This is done when we support sound investments managed by credible companies. We are also saying a lot when we avoid certain companies. Although companies decide on what to do with their own business, involvement of their investors will give a view from the outside looking in. And this is essential for any person, much more when they are dealing with other people's money. A company is, in a nutshell, just a group of people working together for a common objective. As humans, they are still susceptible to mistakes. And one of this is having a narrow view of reality, but inputs from outside will help address this situation.

This is not to say you are to be a nuisance to the insurance provider. Participating merely means speaking to them regarding your own personal experience with their product, service, and delivery. The truth is, even without you speaking, they are observing you! Voicing out your observations just makes clarifies what your nonverbal messages directed toward the company are all about.

Of course you know how adwares are intentionally left in your computer every time your surf the net. Same thing with every product!

Your every choice goes into a little statistical box to note that one more took this product. When you ask questions on how the coffee for the month of Starbucks is prepared, you are actually giving feedback to your barista. Your feedback, along with those of others, is used to concoct the next flavour of the month. You don't have to rely on the adware left in your computer for companies to know your preferences. An active role will actually be better.

WHEN DO I DO THIS?

The time to act is now! Insurance takes your age and health into account. Companies give a rating based on your age, health, and profession. As you advance in age, your premium will rise. The assumption is that people tend to have increasing health concerns as they age. since this is generally true for all people, then there will be less time to make your money grow before you may need to claim some benefit from your policy.

Men are more disadvantage as they advance in age because their premiums are higher than women. So act now. The younger you get an insurance, the better it will be for you.

[1] "National Safety Council Injury Facts 2008 Edition", (IL, USA: National Safety Council, 2008), Accessed November 23, 2014, https://www.usw12775.org/uploads/InjuryFacts08Ed.pdf.

[2] "National Safety Council Injury Facts 2013 Edition", (IL, USA: National Safety Council, 2008), Accessed November 23, 2014, http://www.mhi.org/downloads/industrygroups/ease/technicalpapers/2013-National-Safety-Council-Injury-Facts.pdf.

[3] Elizabeth Warren, "Sick and Broke," *Washington Post* A-23, February 9, 2005.

[4] "Chances of Disability, Council for Disability Awareness," 2012, Accessed November 23, 2014, http://www.disabilitycanhappen.org/chances_disability/.

www.ingramcontent.com/pod-product-compliance
Lightning Source LLC
Chambersburg PA
CBHW070728180526
45167CB00004B/1665